THE AMISTAD REVOLT

ELLIS ROXBURGH

Gareth Stevens
PUBLISHING

Please visit our website, www.garethstevens.com. For a free color catalog of all our high-quality books, call toll-free 1-800-542-2595 or fax 1-877-542-2596.

CATALOGING-IN-PUBLICATION DATA

Names: Roxburgh, Ellis.
Title: The Amistad revolt / Ellis Roxburgh.
Description: New York : Gareth Stevens Publishing, 2018. | Series: Rebellions, revolts, and uprisings | Includes index.
Identifiers: ISBN 9781538207703 (pbk.) | ISBN 9781538207642 (library bound) | ISBN 9781538207529 (6 pack)
Subjects: LCSH: Amistad (Schooner)--Juvenile literature. | Slave insurrections--United States--Juvenile literature. |
   Antislavery movements--United States--Juvenile literature.
Classification: LCC E447.R69 2018 | DDC 326'.80973--dc23

Published in 2018 by
Gareth Stevens Publishing
111 East 14th Street, Suite 349
New York, NY 10003

Copyright © 2018 Gareth Stevens Publishing

For Brown Bear Books Ltd:
Managing Editor: Tim Cooke
Designer: Lynne Lennon
Editorial Director: Lindsey Lowe
Children's Publisher: Anne O'Daly
Design Manager: Keith Davis
Picture Manager: Sophie Mortimer

Picture Credits
Cover: Getty: Library of Congress, Corbis Historical Collection
Interior: France Militaire: Marinet Masson; Gilder Lehrman Institute of American History: 40;
istockphoto: 11; Library of Congress: 7, 9, 21, 25, 26, 30, 32, 35, 39, 43; Metropolitan Museum of Art: 33; NARA: 34,
42; New Haven County Historical Society: 15, 18; Public Domain: Americasroof 24, National Intelligence 37, Research
Archives.gov 31; Shutterstock: Gary Blakeley 36, Everett Historical 4, 5, 6, 8, 12, 13, 16, 17, Slava Gerj 27, Asmus
Koefoed 20, Jerric Ramos 41; Thinkstock: 23, Ingram Publishing 22; Topfoto: The Granger Collection 19; University of
California: 14; Yale University: F.B Carpenter 29, manuscripts & Archives 38.

All other images Brown Bear Books

Manufactured in the United States of America

CPSIA compliance information: Batch #CS17GS. For further information contact Gareth Stevens, New York, New York at 1-800-542-2595.

CONTENTS

WORDS IN THE GLOSSARY APPEAR IN **BOLD** TYPE
THE FIRST TIME THEY ARE USED IN THE TEXT.

ROOTS OF REBELLION

In 1839, African slaves onboard the ship *Amistad* killed the captain and demanded that the ship take them back to Africa. The subsequent legal case changed the course of US history.

Slavery had existed in America since the first African slaves arrived in the English **colony** of Jamestown, in 1619 on board a Dutch slave ship. The early slaves worked alongside **indentured servants** from Europe. These were people who had agreed to do at least 7 years' hard labor in return for their passage to America. But while

→

Slaves process sugarcane on a plantation in Cuba.

indentured servants eventually gained their freedom and even some land, slaves remained slaves. They were the property of their owners, who treated slaves as they wished.

Growing Importance

As the English colonies expanded, they grew rich from exporting tobacco and cotton. Slaves were essential to their economies. As more slaves arrived in America, the few rights the early slaves had were withdrawn. They had no rights and were not recognized as being citizens of any nation.

Slaves wearing shackles arrive in the United States to be sold.

When slavery was legalized in America in 1641, slaves were defined by law as the personal possessions of their white owners. Slaves could be beaten, abused, or even killed without such treatment being considered a crime. For some white owners, slaves were little more than animals.

A Royal Decree

The slaves' position worsened in 1660, when King Charles II of England and Scotland established the Royal African Company. The company built trading ports along the coast of West Africa. From there, slaves who had been seized from farther inland were carried across the Atlantic on slave ships.

A trader prepares to kill a slave on the march to the African coast.

STOWAGE OF THE BRITISH SLAVE SHIP BROOKES UNDER THE
REGULATED SLAVE TRADE
Act of 1788.

Slaves were closely packed beneath the decks of a slave ship. ↑

A Triangular Trade

In the 19th century, European ships sailed to Africa with cargos of manufactured goods. After the goods were sold, slaves were loaded on the empty ships to sail to the Americas. From there, the ships carried raw materials such as timber back to Europe. The three legs earned the journey the nickname of the "triangular trade." The slaves' crossing of the Atlantic was known as the "Middle Passage."

The slaves were put to work on tobacco and cotton plantations in the British-controlled Caribbean Islands and in the American colonies. Slaves were known as "black gold." Their hard work ensured that the colonists grew rich from the goods they exported.

Taken to America

The trip into slavery began when Africans were seized from their villages. Their **kidnappers** were usually Africans working for African or Arab slave traders. The traders targeted healthy young men and women who could work hard.

7

A slave woman is sold at an auction in Richmond, Virginia.

These young slaves would also have children, so they would provide a new generation of slaves. The traders **shackled** their captives together and made them walk to the coast. There, the slaves were held in cells until a slave ship arrived.

The slave ships were overcrowded and **unsanitary**. The slaves were packed in so tightly that they had little room to move. During the crossing, many slaves died from disease, a lack of water and food, or from being harshly punished. Their bodies were thrown over the side of the ship.

Once the ships arrived in the American colonies, the surviving slaves were sold at auctions. Some were put to work inside the house or as craftsmen on estates. Most were sent to labor on plantations.

DID YOU KNOW?

MUCH OF THE COTTON FROM THE SOUTHERN STATES WAS SOLD TO BRITAIN, WHERE COTTON WEAVING TOOK PLACE IN HUGE NEW FACTORIES KNOWN AS MILLS.

Slave owners could choose how harshly or gently to treat their slaves. The law did, however, force them to physically punish any slave who tried to escape.

It is not known exactly how many Africans were forcibly brought to the Americas. Some historians think that as many as 7 million slaves arrived in the 18th century alone.

An Evil Practice

In 1793, Eli Whitney invented the cotton gin. The machine speeded up the manufacture of cotton, so more labor was needed to grow and harvest more cotton. Slavery became central to the economy of the South, where the cotton was grown. Southern cotton and tobacco plantations relied on free slave labor to keep their profits high.

The young slaves brought to the Americas often included children.

Slave Uprisings

In the Caribbean, slaves sometimes rebelled against their owners. Most uprisings were small and easily defeated. A more serious revolt began in 1791 in the French colony of Saint-Domingue, however. It was inspired by the idea of equality for all men. Slaves took over the island. They killed thousands of white people and burned sugar plantations. The slaves eventually founded the independent country of Haiti. The revolt would inspire many other slave uprisings.

→

Slaves kill white French colonists during the revolt on Saint-Domingue.

Meanwhile, opposition to slavery was growing in other parts of the United States and across the world. France abolished slavery throughout its colonies in 1794. After Great Britain lost its American colonies in the American Revolution (1775–1783), a movement grew in Britain to **abolish** slavery. In 1807, the British Parliament passed a law banning the slave trade across the British Empire. In 1833, a further law banished slavery itself throughout all the British colonies, including the Caribbean.

Despite the British ban, the international slave trade continued. In the United States, slavery faced growing opposition. In the industrialized societies of the North, the **institution** was seen as cruel and inhumane. Many northern states outlawed slavery. Slavery would be a major cause of the Civil War that broke out in 1861. Slavery was eventually abolished by President Abraham Lincoln when he issued the Emancipation Proclamation on January 1, 1863.

White overseers with whips watch slaves on a sugar plantation.

WHO WERE THE REBELS?

In January 1839 slave hunters captured hundreds of Africans in Mendeland in present-day Sierra Leone. Mendeland was home to the Mende, one of the two largest ethnic groups in Sierra Leone.

Captive Africans are rowed to a slave ship to be taken to the Americas.

If slaves became sick on the crossing, they were thrown into the sea.

The captives were marched in chains to the coast and sold to a Spaniard named Pedro Blanco. Blanco ran a trading post at the mouth of the Gallinas River in Sierra Leone. He arranged to sell 2,000 slaves even though Spain had outlawed slavery throughout its empire nearly 20 years earlier. The only places where slavery was legal were the islands of Cuba, Puerto Rico, and Santo Domingo, which had sugar and tobacco plantations. This detail later proved key in settling the *Amistad* revolt.

A Brutal Journey

Around 500 African slaves were packed on board a Portuguese ship named the *Tecora*. The ship had been built after the slave trade had been made illegal in Great Britain and Spain.

The *Tecora* was designed to be fast enough to escape from British ships. The Royal Navy patrolled the Atlantic Ocean, trying to intercept ships carrying slaves. There was even less room for slaves on board the *Tecora* than on regular slave ships, which were already overcrowded.

Conditions were terrible. Almost a third of the 500 slaves from Sierra Leone died from disease or starvation during the 10-week journey across the Atlantic. Others died from beatings they received as a form of punishment. When food ran low, the crew threw slaves overboard and left them to drown in the ocean.

Slaves in Cuba unload blocks of ice from a ship.

This is a portrait of Joseph Cinqué, a slave aboard the Amistad.

Reaching Cuba

The ship finally arrived in the port of Havana, Cuba, on June 12, 1839. The slaves who had survived the journey landed in a small bay close to Havana. They were taken ashore on small boats under cover of darkness. It was important they were not seen, because **importing** slaves into Cuba was illegal under Spanish law.

Cheating the Law

The slaves were placed in a pen to await sale. Legally, as soon as they had landed on Cuban soil, they were free citizens. In order to get around the law, the slave traders pretended the Africans had been born into slavery in Cuba. Anyone born into slavery remained a slave. Two Spaniards, Don José Ruiz and Don Pedro Montez, bought 53 of the surviving Africans (49 men, 3 girls, and 1 boy). They planned to sell them to plantation owners on another part of the island.

Ruiz and Montez loaded the slaves on board a ship named *Amistad*. *Amistad* was a regular cargo ship, not a slave ship. It did not have room for all the slaves to be chained below deck as they would be on a slave ship. Half the slaves were locked in the cargo hold. The other half were kept on deck.

Joseph Cinqué

One of the slaves locked in the hold was a Mende named Senge Pieh, later known as Joseph Cinqué (c.1814–1879). When he was taken captive, Cinqué was around 25 years old. He was a rice farmer and the son of a local chief. He may have been seized as punishment for an unpaid debt. Married with three children, Cinqué was a natural leader.

The *Amistad* set sail on June 27, 1839. Onboard with the slaves were seven other men, including Ruiz and Montez and two slaves who worked on the ship, including the cook.

The slaves on the ship were being taken to work on a sugar plantation. ↓

Cinqué's Appearance

The first description of Joseph Cinqué was published in the *New York Journal of Commerce* on August 30, 1839: "On board the brig we also saw Cinqué, the master spirit and hero of this ... tragedy, in irons. He is about 5 feet 8 inches in height, 25 or 26 years of age, of erect figure, well built, and very active. He is said to be a match for any two men on board the schooner. His countenance ... is unusually intelligent, evincing uncommon decision and coolness, with a composure characteristic of true courage, and nothing to mark him as a malicious man."

Planning an Escape

The cook told Cinqué that when they reached their destination, the African slaves would be killed and eaten. Cinqué decided to try to capture the ship. He spoke with some of the other slaves. Some were from different tribal groups, and they spoke different languages. They all managed to agree that they would seize control of the ship if they got a chance.

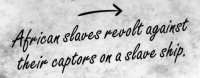

African slaves revolt against their captors on a slave ship.

REBELLION!

Sometime as the *Amistad* sailed along the coast of Cuba, Joseph Cinqué and the other slaves broke free. Their revolt would change the history of the international slave trade.

Amistad was a two-sailed **schooner** that measured around 120 feet (37 m) in length. Its regular cargo was sugar and other products that were shipped between the colonies of the Caribbean islands. On specially built slave ships, all the slaves were kept below decks. They were chained together so tightly

The ship was a fast-sailing schooner used to carry cargo.

The slaves kill Captain Ferrer on the deck of the ship.

that it was difficult for them to move. Because the *Amistad* was not a purpose-built slave ship, however, not all the slaves were able to fit in the hold, and those in the hold with Joseph Cinqué were able to move around quite freely.

Voyage of the *Amistad*

The Spaniards, Ruiz and Montez, had sold the slaves to a sugar plantation in Puerto Principe in the heart of Cuba. They intended to sail along the coast from Havana to a port from where the slaves could be taken inland. On the voyage, Montez acted as **navigator** for the Spanish captain, Ramón Ferrer. Also among the crew were Ferrer's slave Antonio, a slave cook, and two other Spaniards.

According to **contemporary** accounts, the journey was only supposed to have taken 4 days but the ship was delayed by bad weather. On the 5th day, *Amistad* was still at sea. Food and water supplies were running low. The crew decided they would keep what supplies remained for themselves. They would let the Africans starve.

Uncertain Facts

Many of the details of the *Amistad* revolt remain unclear. Some accounts say that it took place on July 1, 1839, and others on July 2. Joseph Cinqué himself later said he could not remember how long after leaving Havana the revolt had begun. It is usually thought that Cinqué freed himself by using an old nail to pick the locks on his shackles, but some versions of the story say he found a file and cut through his chains. Cinqué also claimed that before he killed Captain Ferrer, he gave the ship's captain the opportunity to sail back to Africa. There is no way of knowing if his account is true.

No one knows precisely how Cinqué managed to escape from his shackles.

DID YOU KNOW?

SHACKLES COULD BE USED TO BIND A SLAVE'S FEET OR HANDS, OR BOTH. THE IRON CUFFS RUBBED THE ANKLES AND WRISTS UNTIL THEY BLED.

→

The knives used to cut sugarcane were large and very sharp.

Mutiny!

Realizing they would probably die from hunger, the slaves seized a chance to start their **mutiny**. Joseph Cinqué may have found a loose nail in a deck plank. He hid it and later used it to pick the lock that held the iron **manacles** and shackles around his hands and feet. Some accounts say he cut the shackles with a file he found. He then freed his fellow slaves.

Led by Cinqué, the slaves rushed up from the hold onto the main deck to confront their captors. They were armed with knives for cutting sugarcane, which they had found below deck.

A brief and confused fight followed, during which Ferrer and the cook were killed. Joseph Cinqué is said to have killed the captain himself. Outnumbered, the rest of the crew quickly surrendered to the slaves. The other two Spanish crew members managed to escape in a small rowboat.

FIRST IMPRESSIONS

WHEN THE *Amistad* ENDED ITS VOYAGE IN CONNECTICUT, CITIZENS OF NEW LONDON RUSHED TO THE PORT TO SEE THE SHIP. A REPORTER DESCRIBED THE SCENE: "ON HER DECK WERE GROUPED AMID VARIOUS GOODS AND ARMS, THE REMNANT OF HER ETHIOPIAN CREW, SOME DECKED [DRESSED] IN THE MOST FANTASTIC MANNER, IN SILKS AND FINERY, PILFERED FROM THE CARGO, WHILE OTHERS, IN A STATE OF NUDITY, EMACIATED [THINNED] TO MERE SKELETONS, LAY COILED UPON THE DECKS."

Return Home

Cinqué ordered Ruiz and Montez to sail the ship east, back toward Africa. The Spaniards obeyed his order during the day. During the hours of darkness, however, they deliberately changed the ship's course to the north and west. They hoped eventually to sail close enough to the United States to be rescued.

The *Amistad* remained at sea for the next 2 months. Historians think the ship was zigzagging slowly up the eastern seaboard.

The ship headed east during the day, toward the rising sun.

When the Spaniards took the wheel, they turned the ship to the north. ↑

During the day, Cinqué made sure that Montez was sailing east, toward Africa. The Africans took turns to steer, following the sun. However, any gains they made were lost at night, when the Spaniards turned the ship back toward the north. *Amistad* finally reached land on August 26, 1839. It had not arrived in Africa, however, but at Culloden Point on the eastern tip of Long Island, New York.

Survival at Sea

How did Cinqué and the others on board survive for 2 months? The **provisions** on board the *Amistad* had been running out even before the slaves took over the ship. Accounts report that the *Amistad* met several other vessels. When that happened, Cinqué sent Ruiz and Montez below deck while he traded for food and water. The fact that an African crew had so much money was unusual. The captain of one ship was so suspicious that he followed the *Amistad* for 24 hours. However, no one challenged Cinqué and his crew.

Capture and Imprisonment

The *Amistad* moored up off Long Island while some of the slaves went ashore to buy more supplies. The ship was spotted by the USS *Washington*, a federal **survey** ship. The *Washington*'s captain, Lieutenant Thomas R. Gedney, was

The Amistad moored here off Culloden Point on Long Island. ↓

New Haven Courthouse stood in the center of town.

suspicious of the moored ship. He boarded *Amistad* and freed Ruiz and Montez. He towed the *Amistad* to New London, Connecticut. Slavery was still legal in the state, so Cinqué and the other Africans were arrested as slaves. The Africans were now prisoners of the United States.

Ruiz and Montez told the authorities the Africans were slaves who had not only carried out a mutiny but had also murdered the captain. To make things worse for the Africans, they did not speak English. They did not understand what they were being accused of. Their situation looked bleak.

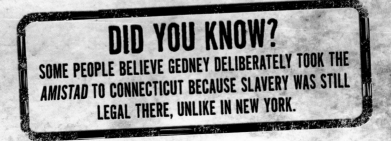

DID YOU KNOW?

SOME PEOPLE BELIEVE GEDNEY DELIBERATELY TOOK THE *AMISTAD* TO CONNECTICUT BECAUSE SLAVERY WAS STILL LEGAL THERE, UNLIKE IN NEW YORK.

FIGHTING AUTHORITY

The Africans from the _Amistad_ were taken into custody and accused of mutiny and murder. If found guilty, they faced execution.

AM I NOT A MAN AND A BROTHER?

On August 29, 1839, the Spaniards Jose Montez and Pedro Ruiz filed a claim of ownership of the Africans as their slaves. The legal situation was complicated, however. The captain of the USS _Washington_, Thomas R. Gedney, was also claiming the slaves under the law of **salvage**, together with the _Amistad_. He may have hoped to sell the slaves and the ship for his own profit.

This pamphlet was produced by Americans who wanted slavery to be abolished. ←

THE LAW OF SALVAGE

Thomas R. Gedney's claim to the Africans on the *Amistad* was based on the law of salvage. Under maritime law, ships' captains were able to claim a share of any goods when they took over a ship to prevent it being lost at sea. This was an ancient tradition. The *Amistad* had not been in peril, however, so the law may not have applied in this case. Also, the Africans said they were the victims of kidnapping, and were not slaves. If they were not merchandise, it followed that they could not legally be claimed as salvage.

If a captain saved a ship from being lost, he was entitled to a share of its cargo.

LEWIS TAPPAN.

At the same time, another court case began. The US authorities charged the slaves from the *Amistad* with mutiny and murder.

By now Cinqué and his companions were being held in a jail in New Haven, Connecticut. Cinqué had been identified as having been the **ringleader**. He was kept separate from the other prisoners so that he could not **incite** any more trouble.

The Friend of Amistad Africans Committee

The plight of the Africans soon attracted the attention of antislavery campaigners. At the time, the **abolitionist** movement in America was growing. Abolitionists called for slavery to be made illegal throughout the United States.

Opponents of slavery were eager to support the *Amistad* mutineers. The abolitionists organized a legal defense for the Africans. They made sure the prisoners had clothes and food, and even provided schooling for the children. They soon formed the Friend of Amistad Africans Committee, usually known as the Amistad Committee.

A Lucky Coincidence

While the *Amistad* Africans were being held in New Haven, they were visited by a Yale professor of ancient languages named Josiah Gibbs. Gibbs was curious about African languages. He got the Africans to teach him the Mende words for numbers. Back in the docks at New York, he was practicing the numbers to himself when an African sailor named James Covey responded. Gibbs took Covey back to New Haven. Covey could speak to many of the Africans and translate their words into English. He became their translator, allowing them to tell their story.

The committee's most influential member was Lewis Tappan, an abolitionist from New York. The most important thing the committee did was to find a **translator** who could speak the Mende language. Now Cinqué and the others could finally tell their side of the story. Cinqué took the role of the group's spokesperson.

→

Josiah Gibbs met a Mende speaker at the docks of New York Harbor.

JOSEPH CINQUEZ.

The brave Congolese Chief, who prefers death to Slavery, and who now lies in Jail in Irons at New Haven Conn. awaiting his trial for daring for freedom.

SPEECH TO HIS COMRADE SLAVES AFTER MURDERING THE CAPTAIN &C. AND GETTING POSSESSION OF THE VESSEL AND CARGO.

"Brothers we have done that which we purposed, our hands are now clean, for we have Striven to regain the precious heritage we received from our fathers. We have only to persevere. Where the Sun rises there is our home, our brethren, our fathers. Do not seek to defeat my orders, if so I shall sacrifice any one who would endanger the rest, when at home we will kill the Old Man, the young one shall be saved, he is kind and gave you bread, we must not kill those who give us water. Brothers, I am resolved that it is better to die than be a white man's slave, and I will not complain if by dying I save you. Let us be careful what we eat, that we may not be sick. The deed is done and I need say no more."

Helped by their supporters, Cinqué and the other African captives responded to the Spaniards' claim on September 19, 1839. They denied ever having been slaves. They were free men and claimed their liberty.

Van Buren's Dilemma

The approaching trial drew attention not only from the abolitionists but also from leading politicians. The Spanish government took the case to the president of the United States, the Democrat Martin Van Buren. He was in a difficult position. An election would take place in 1840. He did not want to lose support through any kind of **controversy**.

Spain demanded that Van Buren hand over the Africans without a trial. Spain claimed that because the Africans were on a Spanish-owned ship, they were Spanish property. If the president ignored the Spanish request, he would anger a regional power with many colonies in the Americas. If he agreed to it, however, he would be seen as having interfered in the legal process. In that case, Van Buren would be seen as going against the separation of powers laid out in the US Constitution, in which the judiciary (the courts) were a separate branch of government from the executive (the president).

If the *Amistad* Africans went to trial and won, however, they would be freed. That would anger slaveowners in the South, who might withdraw their support for Van Buren's re-election in 1840. On the other hand, if the Africans were found guilty, they faced death or permanent slavery, which would anger abolitionists. That might weaken Van Buren's support in the Northeast. The stakes were high.

The Amistad Africans would become the subject of an influential case in the US Supreme Court.

3. The warrant of seizure issued by the said District Court on the 19th of September 1839. and the return of the Marshal thereon.

4. ~~The instruction of the judge of the Circuit Court to the Grand Jury, on the~~

4. The Bills of Indictment filed by the District Attorney against the said Africans for the murder of the Captain and Cook of the Amistad, and also for piracy: and the proceedings of the Grand Jury, and the Instructions of the Circuit Court to the said Grand Jury thereon.

5. The writ of Habeas Corpus in behalf of the said Africans on the said 18th or 19th of Sept. 1839: the return, and the decision of the said Circuit Court thereon

J. Q. Adams.

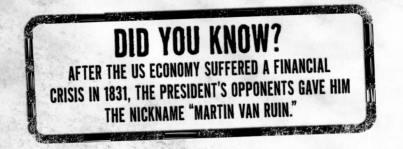

The President Intervenes

In the end, Van Buren decided to return the Africans to Cuba, a Spanish colony. His attorney demanded that they should be handed over to the president so that he could personally return them to Cuba. Justice Smith Thompson of the US Circuit Court heard the request on September 14, 1839. Thompson ruled that, because the mutiny had taken place in **international waters**, American courts had no power to decide what happened to the Africans.

Supporters of slavery argued that plantation life benefited everyone, including slaves.

Van Buren's Attitude

Although Martin Van Buren was opposed to slavery, he also believed slavery was legal under the US Constitution. He had not intended to attack the institution of slavery. He agreed to Spain's request to return the Africans to Cuba in order to gain electoral support in the slave-holding southern states. But if Van Buren hoped to try to resolve the *Amistad* case without causing a controversy about slavery within the United States, he was mistaken.

→

Van Buren made no secret of his personal opposition to slavery.

Helped by their backers, the Africans mounted their own defense. They argued that importing slaves from Africa was illegal under both Spanish law and international treaties Spain had signed. In October 1839, the Africans filed charges against the Spaniards, Ruiz and Montez, accusing them of illegal imprisonment and assault. Ruiz and Montez were ordered to be arrested. Montez escaped to Cuba before he was seized, and after a brief time in jail, Ruiz also fled.

The Spanish ambassador to the United States defended the two men. He argued that Montez and Ruiz should never have

In the matter of the United States Appellants

vs

Cinqua and others severally claimants and appellees

I. Q. Adams, of Counsel for the said Africans, moves the Court for a certiorari to the Judge Clerk of the Circuit Court of the United States for the District of Connecticut, to amend the Record of the proceedings in the said District and Circuit Courts in this case, by sending up copies of the following papers.

1. The proceedings of the Court of Enquiry holden by the honourable Judge of the District Court on board the Schooner Amistad on the 29 of August 1839. and particularly the Indictment against the said Africans for the murder of the captain and mate or cook of the said Schooner. The warrant of seizure issued by the said District Judge on the said 29th of August 1839. directed to the Marshal of the said District, together with the monitions and other process according to law and the return made by the said Marshal made on the 30 of August aforesaid to the said warrant of seizure; and the return to the said monitions.

2. The two warrants of seizure issued by the said District Judge on the 18th of September 1839. and the returns of the Marshal thereon with the process of monition and returns thereon

→

A letter from John Quincy Adams requests documents relating to the case.

been arrested. He repeated the Spanish claim that the whole Amistad case should be thrown out of court. Eventually, the fact that the Spaniards had left America meant they could not testify against the Africans in the court case.

Slow Justice

During the winter of 1839, little happened. Then, in January 1840, the case took a dramatic twist. At the start of the civil trial in the district court, Cinqué and his fellow Africans finally got to explain to a judge what had really happened to them. They told how they had been kidnapped in Africa, sold

John Quincy Adams took on the Amistad case in summer 1840.

in Cuba, and forced into slavery. The judge found the Africans had been illegally sold and ruled that they were free men. He dismissed the charges of murder against them. He ordered Van Buren to send them home to Sierra Leone. The president, however, refused to obey the order. Instead, he ordered an appeal against the ruling. This meant that the case would now be considered by a more senior circuit court.

Van Buren's refusal to follow the court ruling shocked many Americans. The president seemed to be putting support for Spanish interests above those of the United States. Van Buren's popularity fell, but sympathy for the Africans from the *Amistad* grew.

An Important Visitor

In August 1840, the prisoners were moved to a new prison in New Haven. There they met a visitor who would help settle their case. The visitor was John Quincy Adams, the sixth US president (from 1825 to 1829) and the son of the second president, John Adams. John Quincy Adams was a passionate abolitionist who had dedicated his later life to ending slavery.

VICTORY AND LEGACY

With the involvement of John Quincy Adams, the fate of the imprisoned Africans looked more hopeful. The increasingly unpopular US president was now pitched against one of his powerful predecessors.

When abolitionists first asked John Quincy Adams to represent the Africans from the *Amistad* in court, he wondered whether he was up to the task. He was almost blind and busy with his duties as a member of Congress. He was also 72 years old and had not practiced as a lawyer for 30 years. He questioned if he would be as sharp as he had once been.

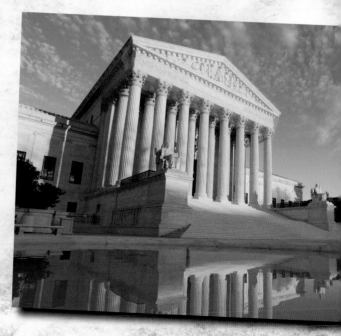

⟶ *The Amistad case ended up in the US Supreme Court.*

The public eagerly followed the case in the newspapers. →

NATIONAL INTELLIGENCER.

THE CASE OF THE AMISTAD.

SUPREME COURT OF THE UNITED STATES.

JANUARY TERM, 1841.

The United States, appellants, *vs.* The Libellants and Claimants of the schooner Amistad, her tackle, apparel, and furniture, together with her cargo, and the Africans mentioned and described in the several libels and claims. On appeal from the Circuit Court of the United States for the District of Connecticut.

Mr. Justice STORY delivered the opinion of the Court:

This is the case of an appeal from the decree of the Circuit Court of the District of Connecticut, sitting in admiralty. The leading facts, as they appear upon the transcript of the proceedings, are as follows:

On the 27th of June, 1839, the schooner L'Amistad, being the property of Spanish subjects, cleared out from the port of Havana, in the Island of Cuba, for Puerto Principe, in the same island. On board of the schooner were the Captain, Ramon Ferrer, and Jose Ruiz and Pedro Montez, all Spanish subjects. The former had with him a negro boy named Antonio, claimed to be his slave. Jose Ruiz had with him forty nine negroes, claimed by him as his slaves, and stated to be his property in a certain pass or document signed by the Governor General of Cuba. Pedro Montez had with him four other negroes, also claimed by him as his slaves, and stated to be his property in a similar pass or document, also signed by the Governor General of Cuba. On the voyage, and before the arrival of the vessel at her port of destination, the negroes rose, killed the Captain, and took possession of her. On the 26th of August the vessel was covered by Lieutenant Gedney, of the United States brig

But Adams had also spent much of his later life fighting against slavery. He realized that the case might be his last act in a long career in public service. Adams agreed to take the case.

In September 1840 he argued the case in front of the US circuit court. His powerful arguments persuaded the court to uphold the earlier decision of the district court.

To the Supreme Court

President Van Buren again refused to accept the court's decision. He ordered the case to be appealed to the US Supreme Court. The case was argued for the government by the Attorney General, Henry D. Gilpin. On February 23, 1841, Gilpin argued that Cinqué and the others were not free men. His argument centered on documents signed by the Governor General of Cuba stating that the men were slaves born in Cuba. As such, Gilpin said, the men were the property of the Spanish government. They must be returned to Spain.

ROGER SHERMAN BALDWIN

BORN IN NEW HAVEN IN 1793, ROGER SHERMAN BALDWIN WAS THE GRANDSON OF ROGER SHERMAN, ONE OF THE FOUNDERS OF THE UNITED STATES. AFTER STUDYING AT YALE, HE BECAME A LAWYER. HE PRACTICED HIS PROFESSION FOR THE REST OF HIS LIFE, EVEN THOUGH HE ALSO SERVED AS A STATE SENATOR, A US SENATOR, AND GOVERNOR OF CONNECTICUT. BALDWIN WAS A NOTED EXPERT ON QUESTIONS OF THE INTERPRETATION OF THE LAW.

Roger Sherman Baldwin kept detailed notes about the Amistad case.

←

The Counterargument

John Quincy Adams was sick, so he could not appear in the Supreme Court. Instead, the argument for the Africans' defense was made by Roger Sherman Baldwin, who had been one of their original lawyers. Speaking for 4 hours, Baldwin argued that the Spanish government was asking for the return of slaves who had been freed by a US court of law. He claimed that the Spanish **petition** ignored the fact that the US courts had already ruled that the men were free men rather than being slaves.

By this time, John Quincy Adams had recovered enough to take up the case. He was an outstanding public speaker and debater and made a powerful argument. He claimed that Van Buren had abused his position to interfere in a judicial decision, and that he had used the presidency to overrule the court. Neither was allowed under the US Constitution.

Adams spoke for 8½ hours. He said that the Africans had been wronged from the moment the *Amistad* was first seized. He criticized the attitudes of both the Spanish monarchy and the US government. He also raised the question about whether the Africans should be treated as people or as **merchandise**. Nobody involved in the case, he said, had been consistent. He argued that the US government was treating the Africans as murderers and mutineers but also as merchandise. So, which were they, he asked.

The Decision

The nine justices retired to consider their verdict on March 2, 1841. A week later, they delivered their verdict. By a majority of seven to one they ruled that the Africans were not slaves. The court ruled that they had been "unlawfully kidnapped, and forcibly and wrongfully carried on board a certain vessel."

Attorney General Henry D. Gilpin argued on behalf of President Martin Van Buren.

A Grateful Letter

Before they left the United States, the *Amistad* Africans wrote a letter to thank John Quincy Adams: "Mende people will remember you when we go to our own country and we will tell all our friends about you and we will say to them Mr. Adams is a great man and he plead for us and how very glad we be and our friends will love you very much because you was a very good man and oh how joyful we shall be."

↑ *John Quincy Adams writes to Roger Sherman Baldwin about the case.*

The highest court in the United States had accepted the version of events put forward by Joseph Cinqué and the other Africans. The original verdict was upheld. The Supreme Court did, however, remove the obligation on Van Buren to return the Africans to Sierra Leone.

Free to Go Home!

Joseph Cinqué and his companions were now free, but they still needed to get home to Mendeland. Abolitionists took them to stay in Farmington, Connecticut, where the Africans were looked after while they waited to return to Africa. The Amistad Committee raised the funds to pay for the journey for those Africans who wanted to go home. Several abolitionists even offered to go with them. They intended to stay in Africa and work as **missionaries**.

A Return Home

Joseph Cinqué and his companions finally arrived in Sierra Leone in 1842. They found the region torn by civil war. Cinqué's own village had been destroyed. He joined his local Christian mission but little is known of his later life. It is known that he left to trade along the coast. Some historians claim that Cinqué became a slave trader himself or that he moved to Jamaica. There is no proof of either story. However, when Cinqué was dying he returned to his mission and asked to be buried as a Christian. He died in 1879.

The justices of the Supreme Court supported the Africans by seven to one. ↓

This paper shows the Supreme Court verdict in the *Amistad* case.

→

Meanwhile, Martin Van Buren went on to lose the 1840 US presidential election to William Henry Harrison. The Spanish government continued to press the United States for compensation for the Africans. The case soured US–Spanish relations for a decade.

Unexpected Consequences

One result of the *Amistad* case was an increase in missionary activity in Africa. The Americans who sailed to Sierra Leone founded a mission in Mendeland. Other members of the Amistad Committee founded the American Missionary Association. Meanwhile, the question of slavery still divided the United States. Eventually, in 1861, it led to Civil War.

DID YOU KNOW?

IN 1997, THE *AMISTAD* MUTINY BECAME THE SUBJECT OF A HOLLYWOOD MOVIE DIRECTED BY STEVEN SPIELBERG ENTITLED *AMISTAD*.

An Example

Henry Highland Garnet was a leading black abolitionist. In a speech he gave on August 16, 1843, Garnet described Joseph Cinqué in terms that set out to make Cinqué a figurehead of the movement: "Joseph Cinqué, the hero of the *Amistad*. He was a native African, and by the help of God he emancipated a whole ship-load of his fellow men on the high seas. And he now sings of Liberty on the sunny hills of Africa, and beneath his native palm trees, where he hears the lion roar, and feels himself as free as that king of the forest."

This Christmas card was sent by US missionaries who went to Africa after the Amistad case.

Christmas Card.

A GIFT TO THE MEMBERS OF THE FOREIGN MISSIONARY BOX ASSOCIATION OF THE PROTESTANT EPISCOPAL CHURCH.

TIMELINE

1791 Slaves revolt on the Caribbean island of Saint-Domingue. They later found the nation of Haiti.

1807 Great Britain bans the slave trade throughout its empire.

1833 The British ban slavery throughout their empire.

1839 **January:** The *Amistad* Africans are among captives seized by slave traders in Sierra Leone.

April: Joseph Cinqué and others are sold and loaded on board the ship *Tecora*.

June 12: The *Tecora* arrives in Cuba, and 53 slaves are sold to José Ruiz and Pedro Montez.

June 27: The 53 slaves leave Havana to sail along the coast in the schooner *Amistad*.

July 1/July 2: Led by Cinqué, the African captives revolt, killing the captain, and ordering the *Amistad* to sail east to Africa.

August 26: Due to trickery by the Spaniards onboard, *Amistad* arrives at Culloden Point on Long Island, New York.

August 29: After the *Amistad* has been taken to New Haven, Connecticut, Montez and Ruiz file a claim to own the Africans.

September: Lewis Tappan founds the Friend of Amistad Africans Committee.

September 14: The case is heard by Justice Thompson in the Circuit Court, and is passed to the District Court.

October: Professor Josiah Gibbs locates a translator named James Covey, allowing the *Amistad* Africans to tell their story. The Africans file a claim against the Spaniards, saying that they are free men, not slaves.

1840 **January:** The district court rules that the Africans should be returned to Africa.

August: Former president John Quincy Adams takes on the case of the *Amistad* Africans.

September: The US government appeals the case to the US Supreme Court.

December 2: President Martin Van Buren loses the election to William Henry Harrison.

1841 **February:** Roger Baldwin and John Quincy Adams argue the case in the US Supreme Court.

March 2: The Supreme Court rules that the Africans should be freed and returned to Africa.

November: The *Amistad* Africans and American missionaries sail for Sierra Leone onboard the *Gentleman*.

1842 **January:** The *Gentleman* arrives in Sierra Leone.

1861 **April 12:** Outbreak of the American Civil War, which is caused partly by tensions over slavery.

1863 **January 1:** Abraham Lincoln's Emancipation Proclamation frees the American slaves.

1879 Death of Joseph Cinqué.

GLOSSARY

abolish: To formally put an end to a practice.

abolitionist: Someone who called for the end of slavery.

colony: A region that is governed by another country.

contemporary: Dating from the same time as something.

controversy: A prolonged public disagreement or argument.

importing: Bringing goods into a country for sale.

incite: To stir up violent or unlawful behavior.

indentured servants: People who work for nothing in return for transportation to a new country.

institution: An established practice.

international waters: Areas of the oceans or seas that lie outside the jurisdiction of any country.

kidnappers: People who seize individuals illegally in order to raise money.

manacles: Cuffs joined by a chain used to fasten a person's hands.

merchandise: Goods that are bought and sold.

missionaries: People who promote a religion, usually in another country.

mutiny: An open rebellion against the officers in control of a ship or part of a military force.

navigator: Someone who plans and follows the course of a journey.

petition: A formal written request to the authorities about an issue.

provisions: Supplies of food and drink for a journey.

ringleader: A person who begins and leads an unlawful activity.

salvage: The rescue of a disabled ship or its cargo from loss at sea.

schooner: A sailing ship with two or more masts.

shackled: Put in chains that fasten the legs or arms

slavery: The state of being owned and forced to work.

survey: The careful measurement of a particular region.

translator: Someone who translates from one language into another.

unsanitary: So dirty or full of germs as to be a danger to health.

FURTHER INFORMATION

Books

Azarian, Melissa Eisen.
The Amistad Mutiny: From the Court Case to the Movie. Famous Court Cases that Became Movies. Berkeley Heights, NJ: Enslow Publishers, 2009.

Baumann, Susan K. **The Middle Passage and the Revolt on the Amistad. Jnr Graphic African American History**. New York: PowerKids Press, 2013.

Gold, Susan Dudley.
United States v. Amistad: Slave Ship Mutiny. Supreme Court Milestones. Tarrytown, NY: Marshall Cavendish Benchmark, 2006.

Grayson, Robert.
Amistad. Essential Events. Edina, MN: ABDO, 2011.

Websites

https://www.archives.gov/education/lessons/amistad
A National Archives page with links to primary sources about the Amistad case.

http://www.ct.gov/kids/cwp/view.asp?a=2573&q=392830
The first part of the Amistad story from the Connecticut state history site for kids.

http://www.ct.gov/kids/cwp/view.asp?a=2573&q=392862
The second part of the story from the Connecticut state history site.

http://www.american-historama.org/1829-1841-jacksonian-era/amistad-incident.htm
An account of the Amistad mutiny for kids, with a list of fascinating facts.

INDEX